MUSIC FOR YOUR WEDDING

MUSIC FOR YOUR WEDDING

PEOPLE'S EDITION

Edited by

Margaret Daly

VERITAS

First published in 1991 by
Veritas Publications
7-8 Lower Abbey Street
Dublin 1
Ireland

Email publications@veritas.ie
Website www.veritas.ie

This edition published in 2004.

ISBN 1 85390 824 X

Acknowledgments
The publishers are grateful to the following for permission to use their copyright material:

Damean Music for 'We Praise you, O Lord' by Mike Balhoff (melody Damean Music); Gerard Keegan for 'Love is Patient'; 'When Love is Found' (Wren/Arr. West) ASCAP, text © Hope Publishing Company and Oxford University Press; Richard Gillard, 'Brother let me be your Servant' (The Servant Song) copyright © 1977 Scripture in Song, administered in Europe by Thankyou Music, PO Box 75 Eastbourne, East Sussex BW23 6NW, UK. Used by permission, 'In perfect charity' © 1982 Randall de Bruyn, published by OCP Publications, 5536 NE Hassalo, Portland, OR 97213. All rights reserved. Used with permission. John L. Bell, 'Blessing for Marriage' and 'Lord and Lover of Creation' from *Love from Below* (Wild Goose Songs Vol. 3), Words © 1989 Iona Community/Wild Goose Publications, Pearce Institute, Govan, Glasgow G51 3UT, Scotland. Barbara O'Hanlon for 'We will live in the Lord'; A.P. Watt Ltd on behalf of *The Grail*, England, for extracts from *The Psalms, A New Translation*, published by William Collins, Sons & Co. Ltd, Sr Pamela Stotter for 'Hymn to Love' (melody and arrangement by David Julien © Edition Fleurus); Máire Ní Dhuibhir for 'Spiorad Dé', 'Fíon agus Uisce' and 'Alleluia as Gaeilge'; Fintan O'Carroll for 'Celtic Alleluia'.

The following are copyright © Margaret Daly

The texts, melodies and arrangements of 'Covenant Song', 'Married to the Lord', 'Wedding Berakah' and 'This is Our Prayer'; the melodies and arrangements of Pss 32(33), 102(103), 111(112), 127(128), 144(145)

The editorial policy has been to choose horizontal inclusive language. The non-inclusive language in 'Love is Patient' has been retained at the request of the composer.

Designed by Paula Ryan
Typesetting by Seton Music Graphics Ltd
Printed in the Republic of Ireland by Betaprint Ltd., Dublin.

Contents

1. WHEN LOVE IS FOUND

1. When love is found and hope comes home,
   Sing and be glad that two are one.
   When love explodes and fills the sky,
   Praise God and share our Maker's joy.

2. When love has flowered in trust and care,
   Build both each day that love may dare
   To reach beyond home's warmth and light,
   To serve and strive for truth and right.

3. When love is tried as loved ones change,
   Hold still to hope though all seems strange,
   Till ease returns and love grows wise
   Through listening ears and opened eyes.

4. When love is torn and trust betrayed,
   Pray strength to love till torments fade,
   Till lovers keep no score of wrong
   But hear through pain love's Easter song.

5. Praise God for love, praise God for life,
   In age or youth, in husband, wife.
   Lift up your hearts, let love be fed
   Through death and life in broken bread.

2. COVENANT SONG

1. God set his heart on us, his beloved,
   He chose us and took us in his care;
   He would be ours and we, his very own.
   So a man sets his heart on a woman,
   She chooses him out of love;
   He will be hers and she, his very own. ℞

Lord,___ how won-der-ful your plan! You give this man and wo-man to each o-ther for life that their hu-man love___ may re-mind___ the world of the stead-fast love of God.___

2. God bound himself to us by a promise,
   A covenant of life and of peace;
   He would be ours and we, his very own.
   So a bride says 'Amen' to her bridegroom,
   He pledges her enduring love;
   He will be hers and she, his very own.

3. God's faithfulness is firm as a mountain,
   His constancy reaches to the clouds;
   He would be ours and we, his very own.
   So a wife will be true to her husband,
   He clings to her in life-long love;
   He will be hers and she, his very own. ℟

Margaret Daly

3. MARRIED IN THE LORD

Margaret Daly

Mar-ried in the Lord, mar-ried in the Lord, may we fol-low him by lov-ing as he loved us. Mar-ried in the Lord, mar-ried in the Lord, may our love grow strong through his power.

1. Christ is the bridegroom
   who came from above
   to win a beautiful bride. ℞

2. Christ is the Friend
   who shared with his own
   all he had learned from the Father. ℞

3. Christ is the lover
   whose love is so great
   that he laid down his life for his friends. ℞

4. Christ is the servant
   who emptied himself,
   accepting death on a cross. ℞

5. Christ is the Lord
   who rose from the dead
   that we might live a new life. ℞

6. Christ is the Head
   who loves us, his Body,
   who nourishes and cares for the Church. ℞

7. Christ is the Bread
   that God gives to us,
   Bread of life for the world. ℞

8. Christ is the Lamb
   whose wedding day has come,
   and all are invited to the feast. ℞

Margaret Daly

4. The Servant Song

1. Will you let me be your servant,
   let me be as Christ to you?
   Pray that I may have the grace to
   let you be my servant too.

3

2. We are pilgrims on a journey,
   we are travellers on the road;
   we are here to help each other
   walk the mile and bear the load.

3. I will hold the Christ-light for you
   in the night time of your fear;
   I will hold my hand out to you,
   speak the peace you long to hear.

4. I will weep when you are weeping;
   when you laugh I'll laugh with you.
   I will share your joy and sorrow
   Till we've seen this journey through.

5. When we sing to God in heaven
   we shall find such harmony,
   born of all we've known together
   Of Christ's love and agony.

6. Will you let me be your servant
   let me be as Christ to you?
   Pray that I may have the grace
   to let you be my servant too.

Richard Gillard

5. LOVE IS PATIENT

1. If I speak with eloquence and baffle all mankind,
   but I am without love, then my speech is blind.
   If I have a vision and understand all things,
   but lack the love of Jesus, I'll miss the joy it brings.

2. If I've faith in fullness to move a mountainside,
   but I am without love, then I'll surely die.
   Let them take my body and burn it on the rack,
   but if I don't love them, there's something else I lack. ℞

Love is pa-tient, love is kind, it is not ar-ro-gant nor rude,—

— it is not re-sent-ful, nor boast-ful, nor jeal-ous, but re-

joi-ces in the truth:___ Love bears all things, be-lieves all

things en-dures what-e-ver comes,___ Love is our hope and

love is our life.___ Love does not come to an end.___

3. Our gifts, they are all transient, they will pass away;
   we have no need for gifts, my friend, at the Judgement Day;
   there's just one thing that we need when we will meet the Lord:
   the greatest gift to all mankind — love is the word. ℟

Gerry Keegan

6. WEDDING SONG

1. Oh let there be songs of joy
   On this our day of days
   And for this feast of life and love
   To God let us give praise.

2. His caring hand has led us here,
   His word unites us now,
   The Christ that once graced Cana's feast
   Will bless our marriage vow.

3. May it be constant with the stars
   With love no flood can drown,
   My love a seal upon your heart
   And yours for me a crown.

4. Now where you go, I will go
   And with you I will dwell;
   In laughter, sorrow, rich or poor,
   For God does all things well.

5. So let there be songs of joy
   On this our day of days,
   And for this feast of life and love
   To God let us give praise.

Liam O'Carroll

7. WE PRAISE YOU, O LORD

Refrain   Darryl Ducote and Gary Daigle

We praise you, O Lord, For all your works are won-der-ful.

We praise you, O Lord, for e - ver is your love.

1. Happy is the home of you that fear the Lord;
   so fruitful shall your love become.
   Your children flourish like the olive plants,
   for ever are you one. ℟

2. May the Lord give you his blessings all your days.
   May you see him fill your land
   until your children bring their children home
   to show his love again. ℟

Mike Balhoff

8. WE WILL LIVE IN THE LORD

We will live in the Lord;
we will love in the Lord
and our life, our strength, our hope will come
from the living God in us.
We will hope in the Lord,
we will glory in the Lord
and our life, our strength, our hope will come
from the living God in us.

One in him, bound in him,
drawing all our life from him,
flower and fruit will abide in him,
in the vine of the living God

So we will live in the Lord;
we will love in the Lord
and our life, our strength, our hope will come
from the living God in us.
We will hope in the Lord,
we will glory in the Lord
and our life, our strength, our hope will come
from the living God in us.

Barbara O'Hanlon

9. WEDDING BERAKAH

Refrain — Margaret Daly

Bless'd are you, O Lord our God, King of the u - ni - verse, giv - er of joy to bride - groom and bride.

1. In your likeness you made both woman and man;
   Blessed are you, O Lord.
   In the image of God you created them;
   Blessed are you, O Lord,
   Female and male you created them;
   Blessed are you, O Lord our God. ℟

2. O fill these dear companions with joy;
   Blessed are you, O Lord,
   As you gladdened the creatures you had made;
   Blessed are you, O Lord,
   In the garden of Eden long ago;
   Blessed are you, O Lord our God. ℟

3. Soon may the streets of Jerusalem ring;
   Blessed are you, O Lord,
   With jubilant sounds of feasting and song;
   Blessed are you, O Lord,
   The voice of the bridegroom, the voice of the bride;
   Blessed are you, O Lord our God. ℟

4. For you have created gladness and joy;
   Blessed are you, O Lord,
   Bride and bridegroom, pleasure, delight,
   Blessed are you, O Lord,
   Unity, fellowship, love and peace;
   Blessed are you, O Lord our God. ℟

Margaret Daly (Text based on the Jewish 'Seven Benedictions')

10. IN PERFECT CHARITY

1. O Most High and glorious God,
   cast your light into the darkness of our hearts.
   Give us right faith, and certain hope,
   and perfect, perfect charity.
   Give us true insight, Lord, and wisdom,
   that we may always live within your ever holy will.
   Lord, may your light within us burn,
   shining out in perfect charity.

2. O Most High and glorious God,
   open wide the door that leads us to your love.
   Give us your firm, yet gentle strength;
   may we live that perfect charity.
   Lord, may your peace be ever in us,
   that we may always seek to serve your people here on earth;
   that we may find our home with you
   and live in perfect charity.

3. Then most high and thankful praise
   we will sing unto the glory of your name:
   to Father, Son and Spirit bright,
   Living Presence, Perfect Charity.
   Praise to the love that shines in splendour,
   that lights the pathways of our hearts and brings us close to you.
   O Holy One, invite us in
   where you live in perfect charity.

   Randall K. DeBruyn (Verse 1 based on a prayer of St Francis of Assisi)

11. O FATHER ALL-CREATING

1. O Father, all-creating,
   Whose wisdom, love and power
   First bound two lives together
   In Eden's dawning hour,
   Today to these your children
   Your earliest gifts renew:
   A home by you kept happy,
   A love by you kept true.

2. With good wine, Lord, at Cana
   The wedding feast you blessed.
   Grant them your saving presence
   And be their dearest guest.
   Their store of earthly treasure
   Transform to heavenly wine,
   And teach them in the testing
   To know the gift divine.

9

3. O spirit, bond of union,
   Breathe on them from above,
   So mighty in your coming,
   So gentle in your love,
   That guarded by your presence
   And kept from strife and sin,
   Their hearts may sense your guidance
   And know you dwell within.

4. Unless you build it, Father,
   The house is built in vain;
   Unless you, Saviour, bless it,
   The joy will turn to pain.
   But nothing breaks a marriage
   Of hearts in you made one.
   The love your Spirit hallows
   Is endless love begun.

John Ellerton 1826–93 (alt.)

12. BLESSING THE MARRIAGE

1. That human life might richer be,
   That children may be named and known,
   That love find its own sanctuary,
   That those in love stay not alone:

Refrain
Margaret Daly

Praise, praise the Mak - er, Spi - rit, Son,
Bles - sing this mar - riage now___ be - gun.___

2. As two we love are wed this day
   And we stand witness to their vow,
   We call on God, the Trinity,
   To sanctify their pledges now. ℞

3. Parents and families they leave,
   Their own new family to make;
   And, sharing what their pasts have taught,
   They shape it for the future's sake. ℞

4. This is as God meant it to be,
   That man and woman should be one
   And live in love and love through life,
   As Christ on earth has taught and done. ℞

John Bell © The Iona Community

10

13. LORD AND LOVER OF CREATION

1. Lord and lover of creation,
   Bless the marriage witnessed now:
   Sign of lives no longer separate,
   Sealed by symbol, bound by vow,
   Celebrating love's commitment
   Made to live and last and grow.

2. Praise and gratitude we offer
   For the past which shaped today:
   Words which stirred and deepened conscience,
   Family life, good company,
   Friends who touched and summoned talent,
   Nourished all words can't convey.

3. On your children wed and welcome
   Here among us we request
   Health in home and hearts, and humour
   Through which heaven and earth are blessed;
   Open doors and human pleasure,
   Time for touch and trust and rest.

4. Take them hence that, in each other,
   Love fulfilling love shall find
   Much to share and more to treasure,
   Such that none dare break or bind
   Those your name has joined together,
   One in body, heart in mind.

John Bell © The Iona Community

14. THIS IS OUR PRAYER

Margaret Daly

Refrain

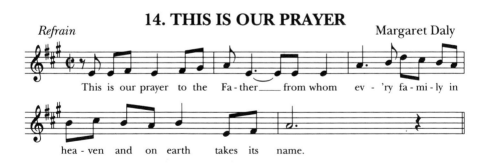

This is our prayer to the Fa-ther___ from whom ev - 'ry fa - mi - ly in hea - ven and on earth takes its name.

11

1. In keeping with the riches of his glory,
   may he strengthen us through his Spirit
   with power in our inmost being
   that through faith Christ may dwell in our hearts. ℟

2. That, rooted and grounded in love,
   we may grasp, with all God's people,
   the breadth, the length, the height
   and the depth of the love of Christ. ℟

3. May we come to know his love,
   though it surpasses all knowledge,
   and so be completely filled
   with the very fullness of God. ℟

4. To him whose power in us
   can go beyond all our hopes and dreams,
   be glory in the Church and in Christ Jesus
   through all generations. Amen. ℟

Singing version of Ep 3:14–21 Margaret Daly

15. SPIORAD DÉ

1. Spiorad Dé ionainn,   *Spirit of God in us;*
   Spiorad Dé tharainn,   *Spirit of God over us;*
   Spiorad Dé ionainn,   *Spirit of God in us.*
   Go bhfógraimís slánú Dé,   *May we proclaim the salvation of God,*
   Síocháin Dé,   *the peace of God,*
   Áthas Dé;   *the joy of God,*
   Spiorad Dé ionainn.   *the Spirit of God in us.*

2. Spiorad Dé ionainn,   *Spirit of God in us;*
   Spiorad Dé tharainn,   *Spirit of God over us;*
   Spiorad Dé ionainn,   *Spirit of God in us.*
   Go leanaimís cosán Dé   *May we follow the path of God,*
   Briathar Dé,   *the word of God,*
   Solas Dé;   *the light of God,*
   Spiorad Dé ionainn.   *The Spirit of God in us.*

3. Spiorad Dé ionainn,   *Spirit of God in us;*
   Spiorad Dé tharainn,   *Spirit of God over us;*
   Spiorad Dé ionainn,   *Spirit of God in us;*
   Go scaipimís Deáscéal Chríost,   *May we spread the gospel of Christ,*
   Sólás Chríost   *the consolation of Christ,*
   Gloír Chríost;   *the glory of Christ;*
   Spiorad Dé ionainn.   *Spirit of God in us.*

4. Spiorad Dé ionainn,   *Spirit of God in us.*
   Spiorad Dé tharainn,   *Spirit of God in us;*
   Spiorad Dé ionainn,   *Spirit of God over us;*
   Go molaimís an tAthair Mór,   *May we praise the great Father,*
   An Slánaitheóir,   *the Saviour,*
   An Cabhróir;   *the Helper,*
   Spiorad Dé ionainn.   *Spirit of God in us.*

Máire Ní Dhuibhir

16. AG AN bPÓSADH BHÍ I gCÁNA

1. Ag an bpósadh bhí i gCána   *At the wedding in Cana*
   Bhí Rí na ngrás ann i bpearsain,   *The King of grace was a guest,*
   É féin is Muire máthair,   *He and Mary, his mother —*
   is nárbh álainn í an bhainis,   *wasn't it a lovely wedding feast!*
   Bhí cuideacht' ós cionn cláirann,   *There was good company at that table,*
   agus fíon orthu in easnamh,   *but the wine ran short.*
   'S an tuisce bhí sna hárthaigh   *And hadn't the water in the vessels*
   nárbh álainn é 'bhlaiseadh.   *a glorious taste?*

2. Is ró-bhreá an stór tá ag   *Very fine is the reward*
   Rí na glóire dúinn i dtaisce,   *which the King of glory has in store for us:*
   A chuid fola agus feola   *His flesh and blood*
   mar lón do na peacaigh.   *as sustenance for us sinners.*
   Ná cuirigí bhur ndóchas   *Place not your trust*
   in ór buí nó i rachmas   *in bright gold or riches*
   Mar is bréagán mar cheo é   *because it is a deception like a fog*
   seachas glóire na bhflaitheas.   *if compared with the glory of heaven.*

Traditional Irish

13

17. FÍON AGUS UISCE

Fíon agus uisce, grá ghníomartha an saoil
Glac leo, a Thiarna, tré Íosa mac Dé.
Críost ós mo chomhair i ngrá ghníomhartha an lae.
Moladh dhuit is móradh tré Íosa mac Dé.
Ár smaointe le grá, ár naigne lách,
ár gcroíthe le báidh do Íosa mac Dé.
In íobairt an ghrá a Thiarna ró-árd,
Glac linn an lá seo tré Íosa mac Dé.

Wine and water, powerful love of humanity,
Accept them, Lord, through Jesus Son of God.
Christ my model in genuine loving each day.
Praise and glory to you, through Jesus, Son of God.
Our loving thoughts, our willing minds,
our hearts full of joy in Jesus Son of God,
in this offering of love, O most glorious Lord (Father),
take possession of us this day through Jesus, Son of God.

Máire Ní Dhuibhir

14

18. HYMN TO LOVE

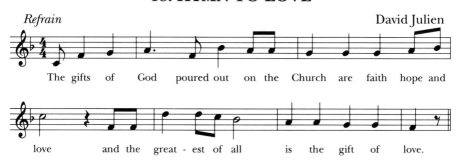

Refrain — David Julien

The gifts of God poured out on the Church are faith hope and love and the great-est of all is the gift of love.

1. For love shows great patience,
   and love meets all needs
   and never envies others,
   always being kind,
   always gentle, always true. ℟

2. And love is not selfish.
   Love is never rude,
   but love brings forgiveness.
   Peace surely dwells
   in the hearts of those who love. ℟

3. And love looks for truth,
   condemning all injustice,
   upholding what is right.
   Love will stand firm
   and love will overcome. ℟

4. Love is filled with hope,
   and love believes all things
   for love endures when all else fails. ℟

Pamela Stotter (based on 1 Co 13:4–13)

RESPONSORIAL PSALMS

1. Psalm 32(33)
THE LORD FILLS THE EARTH WITH HIS LOVE

Refrain   Margaret Daly

The Lord fills the earth with his love.

1. They are happy whose God is the Lord,
   The people he has chosen as his own,
   the Lord looks on those who revere him,
   on those who hope in his love. ℟

2. Our soul is waiting for the Lord.
   The Lord is our help and our shield.
   In him do our hearts find joy.
   We trust in his holy name. ℟

3. May your love be upon us, O Lord,
   as we place all out hope in you. ℟

Ps 32(33):12.18.20-22. R.v.5

2. Psalm 33(34)
TASTE AND SEE THE GOODNESS OF THE LORD

Refrain   Christopher Wilcock

Taste and see the good-ness of the Lord; taste and

see the good-ness of the Lord.

1. I will bless the Lord at all times,
   his praise always on my lips:
   in the Lord my soul shall make its boast.
   The humble shall hear and be glad. ℟

2. Glorify the Lord with me.
    together let us praise his name.
    I sought the Lord and he answered me;
    from my terrors he set me free. ℟

3. Look towards the Lord and shine with light;
    let your faces not be abashed.
    When the poor cry out, the Lord hears them
    and rescues them from all their distress. ℟

4. The angel of the Lord is encamped
    around those who revere him.
    Taste and see that the Lord is good.
    They are happy who seek refuge in him. ℟

                                    Ps 33(34):2–9.R. v.9

3. Psalm 102(103)
YOUR LOVE NEVER FAILS THOSE
WHO REVERE YOU, LORD

Refrain   Margaret Daly

Your love ne - ver fails those who re - vere you, Lord.

1. My soul, give thanks to the Lord;
    all my being, bless his holy name.
    My soul, give thanks to the Lord
    and never forget all his blessings. ℟

2. The Lord is compassion and love,
    slow to anger and rich in mercy.
    As parents have compassion on their children,
    the Lord has pity on those who fear him. ℟

3. The love of the Lord is everlasting
    upon those who hold him in fear:
    his justice reaches out to children's children
    when they keep his covenant in truth. ℟

                        Ps 102(103):1–2.8.13.17–18. R.v.17

4. Psalm 111(112)
HAPPY ARE THOSE WHO TAKE DELIGHT IN THE LORD'S COMMANDS

Refrain   Margaret Daly

Hap - py are those who take___ de - light in the Lord's com - mands.

1. Happy are those who fear the Lord,
   who take delight in all his commands.
   Their descendants shall be powerful on earth;
   the children of the upright are blessed. ℟

2. Riches and wealth are in their homes;
   their justice stands firm for ever.
   They are lights in the darkness;
   they are generous, merciful and just. ℟

3. Good people take pity and lend,
   they conduct their affairs with honour.
   The just will never waver,
   they will be remembered for ever. ℟

4. They have no fear of evil news;
   with firm hearts they trust in the Lord.
   Open-handed they give to the poor;
   their justice stands firm for ever. ℟

Ps 111(112):1–9.℟ cf.v1

5. Psalm 127(128)
SEE HOW THE LORD BLESSES THOSE WHO FEAR HIM

Refrain   Margaret Daly

See how the Lord bles - ses those who fear him.

1. O blessed are those who fear the Lord
   and walk in his ways. ℟

2. By the labour of your hands you shall eat.
   You will be happy and prosper;
   the wife will be like a fruitful vine
   in the heart of the house;
   children like shoots of the olive
   around the table. ℟

18

3. Indeed thus shall be blessed
those who fear the Lord.
May the Lord bless you from Zion
all the days of your life!
May you see your children's children
in a happy Jerusalem!
On Israel peace! ℟

Ps 127(128):1–5. R.cf v4

6. Psalm 144(145)
HOW GOOD IS THE LORD TO ALL

Refrain   Margaret Daly

How good is the Lord, how good is the Lord to all.___

1. The Lord is kind and full of compassion,
   slow to anger, abounding in love.
   How good is the Lord to all,
   compassionate to all his creatures. ℟

2. All your creatures shall thank you, O Lord,
   and your friends shall repeat their blessing.
   The eyes of all creatures look to you
   and you give them their food in due time. ℟

3. The Lord is just in all his ways
   and loving in all his deeds.
   He is close to all who call him,
   who call on him from their hearts. ℟

Ps 144(145):8–10.15.17–18.R. v.9

7. Psalm 148
ALLELUIA, PRAISE THE LORD FROM THE HEAVENS

Refrain   David Julien

Al - le - lu - ia, al - le - lu - ia, al - le - lu - ia.

1. Praise the Lord from the heavens,
   praise him in the heights, alleluia.
   O praise him, all his angels,
   praise him all his host, alleluia, alleluia. ℟

2. Praise the Lord, sun and moon,
   praise him, shining stars, alleluia.
   O praise him, highest heavens
   and waters in the heavens, alleluia, alleluia. ℞

3. All the mountains and hills,
   all fruit trees and cedars, alleluia,
   all beasts wild and tame,
   all birds on the wing, alleluia, alleluia. ℞

4. All earth's peoples and kings,
   the princes and rulers, alleluia,
   the young men and the maidens,
   the old and the children, alleluia, alleluia. ℞

5. May the Lord's name be praised,
   his name and no other, alleluia,
   for greater is his name
   than heaven and earth, alleluia, alleluia. ℞

Adapted from Psalm 148

8. Salm 148
ALLELUIA, MOLAIGÍ AN TIARNA Ó NA FLAITHIS

Freagra   Máire Ní Dhuibhir

Al - le - lu - ia,   al - le - lu - ia,   al - le - lu - ia.

1. Molaigí an Tiarna ó na flaithis
   Molaigí sna hárda é
   Molaigí é, a aingle uile leis,
   Molaigí é, a armshlua uile leis. **Fr.**

   Praise the Lord from the heavens,
   praise him in the heights,
   praise him, all his angels,
   praise him all his host.

2. Molaigí é, a ghrian is a ghealach,
   Molaigí é, a réaltaí soilseacha uile,
   Molaigí é, a fhlaitheasa na bhflaitheas,
   agus a uiscí atá ós cionn na bhflaitheas.
   Fr.

   Praise him, sun and moon,
   praise him, shining stars.
   Praise him, highest heavens
   and the waters above the heavens.

20

3. A shléibhte agus a chnoca uile,   *All mountains and hills,*
   A chranna toraidh agus a chranna   *all fruit trees and cedars,*
        céadrais go léir,
   A ainmhithe allta agus a bheithigh uile, *beasts wild and tame,*
   a phiasta agus a éanacha eiteacha. **Fr**. *reptiles and birds on the wing.*

4. Ríthe na cruinne is na pobail uile,   *All earth's kings and peoples,*
   Flatha is breithiúna uile na cruinne,   *earth's princes and rulers,*
   ógánaigh agus maighdeana,   *young men and maidens,*
   seanóirí agus leanaí. **Fr**.   *the old together with children.*

5. Molaidís ainm an Tiarna   *Let them praise the name of the Lord*
   mar is é ainmsean amháin atá ardaithe *for he alone is exalted.*
   Sáraíonn a mhaorgacht   *The splendour of his name*
   Talamh agus neamh.**Fr**.   *reaches beyond heaven and earth.*

Salm 148:1-4, 9-14

GOSPEL ACCLAMATIONS

1. ALLELUIA

Howard Hughes

Al - le - lu - ia, al - le - lu - ia, al - le - lu - ia, al - le - lu - ia.

Verse: If we love one another,
       God will live in us in perfect love.   (*1 Jn 4:12*)

Alternative verses:

1.   God is love:
      let us love one another
      as God has loved us.   (*1 Jn 4:8.11*)

2. As long as we love one another,
   God will live in us
   and his love will be complete in us.   (*1 Jn 4:2*)

3. All who live in love
   live in God,
   and God lives in them.   (*cf 1 Jn 4:16*)

4. Everyone who loves
   is begotten by God,
   and knows God.   (*1 Jn 4:7*)

During the season of Lent the following acclamation replaces the alleluia:

Howard Hughes

Glo - ry to you, Word — of God, Lord Je - sus Christ!

2. CELTIC ALLELUIA

Fintan O'Carroll

Al - le - lu - ia, al - le - lu - ia,

al - le - lu - ia, al - le - lu - ia.

Verse: All who live in love
           make their home in God,
           and God remains in them.   (*cf 1 Jn 4:16*)

Alternative verses:

2. If we love each other
   God will live in us
   in full-grown, perfect love.   (*cf 1 Jn 4:12*)

22

3. Every one who loves
becomes a child of God
and learns to know the Lord. (*cf 1 Jn 4:7*)

4. God is love;
so let us love each other
since God loved us so much. (*cf 1 Jn 4:8.11*)

During the season of Lent the following acclamation replaces the alleluia:

Fintan O'Carroll

Praise to you, Lord Je - sus Christ, King of end - less glo - ry. Praise to you, Lord Je - sus Christ, King of end - less glo - ry.

3. FOLK ALLELUIA

Christopher Walker

Al - le - lu - ia, ___ al - le - lu - ia al - le - lu - ia, ___ al - le - lu - ia, al - le - lu - ia, ___ al - le - lu - ia al - le - lu - ia, ___ al - le - lu - ia.

Verse: God is love,
if God loved us so much,
we must have the same love for one another. (*cf 1 Jn 4:8.11*)

Alternative verse: All who live in love
live in God
and God lives in them. (*cf 1 Jn 4:12*)

4. SEINN ALLELUIA

Irish Traditional

Seinn al - le - lu - ia, Seinn al - le - lu - ia, Seinn

al - le - lu, seinn al - le - lu, Seinn al - le - lu - ia.

Verse: God is love;
and as long as we love one another,
God will live in us in perfect love. (*cf 1 Jn 4:8.12*)

Alternative verses:

1. God is love;
    let us love one another
    as God has loved us. (*1 Jn 4:8.11*)

2. As long as we love one another,
    God will live in us,
    and his love will be complete in us. (*1 Jn 4:12*)

3. All who live in love
    live in God,
    and God lives in them. (*1 Jn 4:16*)

4. Everyone who loves
    is begotten by God,
    and knows God. (*1 Jn 4:7*)

5. An té a thugann grá
    is ó Dhia a rugadh é
    agus aithníonn sé Dia. (*1 Eoin 4:7*)

6. An té a mhaireann sa ghra,
    maireann i nDia
    agus maireann Dia ann. (*1 Eoin 4:16*)

5. ALLELUIA AS GAEILGE

Máire Ní Dhuibhir

Al - le - lu - ia, al - le - lu - ia, al - le - lu - ia._____

Verse: An té a thugann grá
            is ó Dhia a rugadh é,
            agus aithníonn se Dia. (*1 Eoin 4:7*)

Alternative verse:
            An té a mhaireann sa ghrá
            maireann i nDia
            agus maireann Dia ann. (*1 Eoin 4:16*)

Music For Your Wedding is a timely resource which contains thirty songs and hymns in various musical styles: contemporary liturgical songs with organ, piano and/or guitar accompaniment, hymns, traditional Irish melodies with texts in English arranged for keyboard and for small ensembles (for example Irish harp, flute and violin), and Irish language settings. There are biblical canticles and psalms (including the special responsorial psalms provided in the Lectionary for the celebration of marriage), a Jewish blessing prayer and modern compositions.

This collection will encourage solo singers at weddings to exercise their liturgical ministry as cantors, that is, to sing the verses and invite the congregation to sing the refrains.

Music For Your Wedding can also be used during pre-marriage courses. Couples could be given the people's edition and invited to listen to the cassette tapes together. This would challenge them with a rich and attractive presentation of the great themes of the sacrament which they are about to celebrate: covenant, fidelity, marriage 'in the Lord', the great commandment of love, the bond of the Spirit and the providence of God in their lives.

ISBN 1-85390-824-X

9 781853 908248

www.veritas.ie

The
Sixfold
Path

Six Simple Exercises for
Spirital Development

JOOP VAN DAM